Your Guide
To DEBTS And
REFINANCING

James M.

Table of contents

Introduction

This e-book will help you understand the importance of debt management and how responsible refinancing can help you. It describes various types of debt and helpful information that can assist you with making important financial decisions.

Managing your debts is something you need to do in order to get through today and plan for tomorrow and the earlier you improve your money management skills the sooner you can reach your goals in life.

This tone of this book assumes that you are either in debt or trying to prevent debt difficulties and looks at various areas of finance including:

- Credit ratings
- Types of debt
- Keeping debt manageable before it gets out of control
- Debt reduction
- Identity theft

- Credit cards
- Lines of credit
- Payday loans
- Interest rates
- Late fees
- Loans
- Mortgages
- Refinancing
- Debt consolidations
- Dealing with creditors
- Reducing your debt
- Repossession
- Foreclosure
- Creditor harassment
- Bankruptcy
- Budgeting

This book is also a great guide for those first starting out on their own. By knowing how to manage your finances and learning from the mistakes of others, you can have a concrete plan in place for your financial future.

Finances and Relationships

It's difficult to manage finances on your own but it can be even more difficult when you are in a relationship with someone else and the finances are shared. Approaching money with common goals and expectations is important. Both people in a relationship should understand how the family's financial situation looks. Being in the dark about your finances and letting your partner handle them could not only be dangerous for your financial future but if for any reason you are suddenly in a position where you need to manage the finances, it could feel like being thrown head first into a fire. If you're not in the know about your money, you need to sit down and have a good look at it.

Money is considered the top source of marital problems and separation. Tackling your finances together, even if they don't look pretty is difficult. This book will help you do that.

Finances and Their Impact on Your Health

Your finances shape your present and your future so responsibly managing them is vital to your health and well being. Not only is debt bad for your future but also it's bad for your health. Being in debt can create an enormous amount of stress and impact health.

Making a plan to tackle your finances

If you're in debt, refinancing can be a way to help you get out but only if it's done properly and only if you change your spending habits. This book is going to provide you with information about your debts and help you recognize how debts can spiral out of control. It also looks at various ways to get your spending under control so that you can plan effectively for your future.

Getting out of Debt = Breaking Free of A Big Ball and Chain!

While debtors no longer have to go to work houses or debtors prison, being in debt can be something that feels like being enslaved. The stress can affect every area of your life and can hurt your relationships, your marriage, your health and your employability.

If you are in a position where you have trouble making all your bill payments on time and have no emergency fund or nest egg for the future, this e-book can help you change that by getting you informed, helping you see where you could make changes in your finances and by giving you practical information to help you whether it means refinancing, bankruptcy or changing your spending habits with setting a new budget and debt repayment plan.

Disclaimer:

This e-book contains subjective material provided for informational purposes and does not guarantee that advice or information described in this book will cause or create financial gain or financial loss. The information contained in this book may or may not help you in your own finances.

The publisher of this book will not be held responsible or liable for any financial gain or loss resulting from information contained in this e-book. Always invest and borrow responsibly.

1

Good Debts / Bad Debts

This chapter looks at the fact that there are many types of debts but specifically you can take most types of debts and put them into two silos.

There are good debts and bad debts.

In today's world, we sometimes need the ability to buy something on credit. Learning about identifying positive and negative debts can help you make solid financial decisions so that credit is used wisely.

Types of Debts

Debts are something that most people have to contend with today. Gone are the days of simply paying cash for everything you want. Because of credit cards, loans and mortgages we can buy something now and pay for it later.

The buy now / pay later mentality can be dangerous.

Credit card and loan companies charge interest rates and late payments and they can make it very easy for us to become imprisoned by our debt. In fact, many creditors do their best to make credit easy to get so people will use it.

After all, the longer we take to pay our debts, the more interest we pay and the more interest we pay, the wealthier the creditors become.

This can be dangerous if you act impulsively and don't carefully watch where your money is going. Many people have multiple bad debts, which can amount to financial hardship quickly if it's not kept in check.

Again, there are good debts and bad debts. Not all debts are negative.

Good Debts

In a nutshell, a good debt will net you something at the end of paying for it and a bad debt is something that costs you extra. An illustration of a good debt is a house that costs you 6% interest to finance but that allows you to sell at a profit of 20%. This is a good debt. It's also good because you can live in it while you are paying for it.

Borrowing money to go to college or university is considered a positive debt because it will result in you having something very valuable. Although you pay interest, you will have an education that will boost your income and result in a higher quality of life.

Another good debt would be to borrow money that could create more money for you such as with a loan to buy investment products where the amount the investment pays is higher than the loan interest rate.

Borrowing money to get a tax advantage such as with certain retirement investments can also be considered a good debt. Credit used wisely can also create a positive credit rating, which can help you qualify for good credit products down the road that can increase your wealth.

The Problem

The problem with some types of credit is that it is designed to promote overspending. Advertising in general promotes overspending as convenient. When people use their credit cards to live on and only pay the minimum balance each month, the interest rates compound and it becomes very difficult to get out of debt.

The Solution

Investing in good credit as much as possible and working to avoid or eliminate bad credit will help you.

Bad Debts

Bad debts result in you paying more for something than it is worth. You'll often see ads that defer payments until a later date. This can work to your benefit if you pay by that date. Many advertisements will defer payments for a year but on the 366th day will charge a very high interest rate. Unless you pay for that item in full on day 365 or sooner, you'll pay more for the product than it's worth. The creditor tells you that you can pay in a year for no extra fee but they are really hoping that you will take longer to pay so they can earn interest from you.

This is why these types of debts are opened with a credit card. A furniture store, for instance will give you a store credit card and a "Don't Pay For A Year" deal and on day 366 you will get a credit card statement with a high interest rate.

Many creditors who offer these types of payment plans also inflate their prices so that they make ever more money because they charge you a high fee for the product and make even more money when you elect to make minimum monthly payments instead of paying the balance in full.

Cash advances from credit cards are a similar bad debt. If you borrow cash from your credit card, you'll pay more interest than otherwise. This is another example of a bad debt. It might be convenient to borrow cash from your credit card but you might really be borrowing double when you factor in the interest rate because you don't pay for it right away and just send in the minimum monthly payment at the end of the month.

Many credit cards tack these transactions onto the end of your statement and don't bump it ahead of transactions that charge lower interest rates so your payments won't even touch that transaction and it takes longer to pay back that debt.

Some bad debts are unavoidable. A car loan is a good example of this. When you buy items with credit that will depreciate before you've paid for them, this is negative. A car is an item you might need to finance due to lack of cash so while it seems like it shouldn't be a bad debt, it's not a good investment to make on credit. If you shop around for the right car loan at a low interest rate it reduces the sting.

Can you turn a bad debt into a good debt?

Yes, you can – with refinancing. The right refinancing deal can save you money and turn a bad debt into a debt that's not as bad because it can get you debt free sooner and at a lower cost.

Bad Debts Can Try to Masquerade as Good Credit

Don't be fooled! Some bad debts try to masquerade as good deals and sometimes areas become grey and blurred. You need to be careful.

It might be a good idea to take a home equity loan to improve that home and increase the value but if you strip your home's equity in order to relieve other debt, this isn't as good. It depends on many factors including the interest rate and whether or not you use that as an opportunity to change some spending habits.

Some department stores will offer you a ten per cent or twenty per cent discount on your first purchase if you apply for their store credit card. This is not a good debt, as those cards tend to have the highest interest rates around so after your initial purchase, unless you plan to pay your balance in full each month, a store credit card is not typically good credit.

Some banks will offer introductory rates as well on credit cards. Always read the fine print! That introductory offer might sound great today but don't forget to calculate the rate after the intro period has passed.

The Importance of Managing Debts

Managing your debts is the key to financial success and financial solvency. Living above your means is equal to a bad cycle of debt. Living at your means is more desirable but living below your means is ideal because you are successful with money this way and can increase your buying power.

Buying with cash has many benefits that you can take advantage of. We'll discuss this later on in more depth but money is a powerful tool when you use it effectively.

Living at or below your means takes power away from you and can have a really negative impact on your future.

How do you manage debts?

The key to money management is to spend effectively, save money and plan.

- **Spend Effectively**
  Spend carefully. Live on a budget and for major purchases, do comparison-shopping so you're getting value for your money.

- **Save Money**
  Save for a rainy day. For every dollar you earn, a certain percentage should go to savings. Whether you put it in a high interest bank account or invest it or even better, do a bit of both; saving money is

the only way to have financial freedom. Don't let your debts enslave you!

- **Plan for Your Future**
  Make short term and long-term financial goals. Today a goal might be to pay off your credit cards. Tomorrow you might have a plan to buy a house or a vacation property or simply save for a vacation.

Setting goals and measuring your rate of success, as part of your own financial plan is important. Planning for your financial future with savings and investments is something people should do. Far too many people are living paycheck to paycheck and increasing their debt ratio annually by double-digit numbers.

2
Credit Reports 101

This chapter looks at the importance of credit ratings and how they can affect your life and ability to do what you want. Today, your credit rating can even have an impact on your ability to get the job that you want.

This chapter will help you:

- Understand what creditors and lenders use the credit report for,
- How your credit rating might be impacted and
- Helps you learn ways to improve your credit rating.

The credit rating is an excellent tool for determining how you look to potential lenders and it's a good idea to review credit reports for yourself at least annually and maybe even more regularly if you are currently working to fix what looks bad and up your credit score.

What is a Credit Report?

Credit reports have been gathered for many generations although they haven't always been so easily looked at. In the early 1800's the first third party credit reporting agencies were formed in order to provide a service of reporting on credit history. Today there are several companies that do credit reporting such as Equifax who is the most common agency in the U.S and Canada as well as the United Kingdom.

What is a credit rating or credit report?

There are credit reports for businesses and for consumers. A consumer credit report system provides information on a person's credit history. Many financial transactions can impact your credit report including:

- Loans and mortgages
- Major credit cards
- Utility bills
- Payday loans
- Store credit cards
- Government tax issues

Information about what your debts are, what your debt repayment history is and other information about you is available for lenders who read it to make a decision about whether or not to grant you credit. The information is updated continually. Information that includes employment history, contact information and public records and disputes are also listed.

Not all lenders view credit reports the same way. Some look for stellar credit before they will approve a credit application and some look at various aspects to help them determine overall creditworthiness and ability to repay the debt.

Some people with a blemished credit rating will get access to credit at a higher interest rate or with a co-signor or collateral and some creditors will not deal with someone with bad revolving debt.

What can impact your credit report?

Not only will not paying a bill on time (or at all) hurt you as well as late payments and wage garnishments or court judgments but even inquiries on your account can also affect your ability to get credit.

Your own inquiries on your report won't hurt you. In fact, this knowledge will help you. It's a good idea to check your credit report regularly for errors, omissions, and signs of identity theft and to see how you measure up to potential creditors. Many people who have trouble getting a loan or qualifying for a mortgage are given the recommendation of working to improve the look of their credit report.

Getting a Copy of Your Credit Report

Your credit report is available to you free of charge if you request it. There are services that offer to expedite it for a fee but you can request it on your own and have a copy mailed to you so that you can check and see what the listings are.

Companies like Equifax will supply you with a mailed copy free of charge if you send in a form indicating that you want your credit report and supply proof of identity to them. You can also order an instant report for a fee from their websites.

If you obtain your credit history and you don't like what you see, you will want to act on it. Be careful about acting on it though; many sharks are out in the sea looking to people who want a better credit report as prey.

Credit Repair Services

There are services that will offer for a fee to fix your credit report. In truth, the only things that can be removed from your report are errors. If you dispute something on your report you need to contact the credit bureau reporting agency and notify them. You may choose to have help from your financial planner or lawyer in dealing with complex issues but be very wary of anyone who claims that they can have bad debts removed from your report.

Just because something is listed with a negative on your credit report doesn't mean you have to live with it. If you pay a debt, you may be able to get your lender to agree to remove a poor rating. Negotiation can work in your favor if you talk to them in advance. Even if they refuse to remove their negative report about you, it's still worthwhile to negotiate your debts because sooner or later the report will disappear from your credit history.

Other Information About Your Credit Report

How long information stays on your report depends on where you live. In some areas, records remain on the report for between four and seven years depending on the type of debt. Some systems have a coding system that indicates the status of a debt including whether you're in credit counseling, how many times you've had a late payment and whether or not the debt is a revolving bad debt. Some other areas and programs use a score.

Your Beacon score, Emperica Score, FICO Score or Pinnacle Score can affect the interest rate you are charged and whether or not you qualify for a loan or credit card. Although your credit report may be the same across different credit reporting agencies, your score could be different and is devised using a specific formula and algorithm.

Identity Theft

Identity theft is a growing concern in this digital age. Thieves can have loans and credit cards created in your name and this can have a very negative impact on your credit report.

Many people discover an identity theft when they are declined for credit because they look closely at their credit report. This demonstrates that there are good reasons to look at your report proactively instead of waiting until you need credit and are declined.

If your report has any errors or you are the victim of identity theft, the authorities can launch an investigation and help you have things put right again. Be very careful about sharing your personal details with anyone, especially online. Identity thieves often use the Internet to steal information that lets them print false identification and obtain fraudulent credit.

Improving your Credit Report

The two things that can improve your credit report are:

1. Effort
2. Time

Over time you can rebuild your credit slowly by paying your bills on time and choosing credit products that you know will improve your credit history. Your past errors will eventually be removed and good behaviour will start to overshadow your past mistakes.

If you don't want to wait for four or seven years, you can take action to help increase your score. Some services offer a high interest loan to people with poor credit histories with security and this will result in positive reporting to your report as you make payments on time. Or, pre-paid credit cards do the same thing. You pay a higher interest rate but regular payments will be reported to the credit bureaus, which will help your credit score over time.

Using these services will cost a fee and are advisable only when you are in a good financial position. For instance, a loan might be taken solely for correcting credit payments and the funds left in an interest bearing account to pay for the payments. The worst thing you can do in a "bad credit" position is to default on yet another loan or have another item repossessed. Be careful of "Poor or No Credit" offers because very often they are for things that become unaffordable which decreases your ability to make the payment.

Paying off old debts could result in fixing your credit as well. Some creditors will agree to remove their negative scoring from your report if you settle your account.

3

Credit Cards

Credit cards are very popular. Many say that they're essential. Having one can enable you to shop without cash, buy something in an emergency and reserve things such as hotel rooms, car rentals and airplane tickets. Some companies require a credit card as security to do things so you might find life difficult if you don't have one.

More than that, they're a convenience. You can buy something now and pay for it later. Because of this, you need to be responsible about credit cards. Most cards have a limit and a set of interest charges and membership fees for your use. Be aware of the various fees and how much having a credit card actually costs you.

Because credit cards are almost as good as cash, it can be easy to use them just about anywhere and because you don't see the money leaving your hands, it's easy to overspend.

This chapter will help you learn about credit cards, credit card dangers and about ways you can use them to help you instead of hurt you.

How to get a credit card

You can get a credit card from your bank, credit union or trust company or through a financial company that sells credit cards. This refers to traditional credit cards with a credit limit and an associated interest rate.

There are also pre-paid gift credit cards but we'll discuss that later on in this chapter.

When you apply for a credit card, you need to give personal details about your financial situation and your employment situation. Credit card companies will review your application and look at things such as your debt ratio and your credit history and credit score.

Having a good report can result in your getting qualified for a higher credit limit and a lower interest rate. People with blemished histories might still qualify for a credit card but may be given a low credit limit and / or a high interest rate plus fees. They may also be offered a pre-paid credit card to help them rebuild their credit.

You can apply to credit card companies online (carefully of course, to protect your personal details.) and when opening a new bank account, a financial institution may run your credit history to see if they can offer you a credit card.

Types of Credit Cards

Not all credit cards are created equally. There are many options available and many companies who have differing rules about policies and interest charges and membership fees so if you have a good credit history you can shop around for a great card with low fees. You can also use negotiation power with credit card companies but we'll discuss that later in the book.

To get you interested in their card, a bank or financial services company might offer a low introductory rate. Be aware of what the rate will be in the long term and how it can impact your ability to make payments.

Major Credit Cards

Major credit cards like Visa, MasterCard and American Express are the standards in the industry. There are other major cards as well but these are the most common and can be available from many different institutions. They are widely accepted and have an assigned interest rate plus an assigned limit.

No Limit Credit Cards

There are credit cards without a posted spending limit. These are not easy to get but are often used by very wealthy people and by companies who need a large amount of available credit.

Store Credit Cards

Store credit cards can be used at a particular store. These cards tend to have the highest interest rate. If you use these cards and pay the full balance, they are not different than cash and could have loyalty programs or other convenience reasons but when interest starts to accumulate, things don't look so great on paper.

Line of Credit

A revolving line of credit looks like a credit card and lets you take money out or use it for Debit purchases. The line of credit may be secured or unsecured. It's often secured against a mortgage. This is a flexible way to borrow and is similar to having a pre-approval for a specific amount that you can take when you need it.

Prepaid Credit Cards

A prepaid credit card has a credit card company's logo but is more of a debit card or a akin to a gift card. Some prepaid credit cards are used like a credit card but do nothing but offer a cashless option. Other prepaid cards are designed to help you re-establish your credit rating and require you to pre-pay for the credit limit you desire and pay an interest fee to use it. Credit card companies that offer this service typically do so with the promise of reporting your activity frequently. Making regular payments can help you improve and re-establish your credit rating.

Credit Card Dangers

Credit cards can be very convenient but they can carry dangers. Credit card debt is considered among the most serious debts because the card accumulates interest and fees quickly and because it's as easy to spend as money.

Many experts say it's much easier to overspend when you use a credit card because you don't think about the consequences because it doesn't feel like spending real cash. This is dangerous.

The problem with credit cards is the accumulating compound interest. Not only do you pay interest on your purchases but also you pay interest on top of your interest. Unless you make a full payment each month and leave no balance, you will be paying more for the items you buy with a credit card than you would if you pay with cash.

Cash Advances

Cash advances are particularly dangerous because most credit card companies don't wait until the due date after the statement has been issued to begin charging you interest. They often charge interest from the day you take the cash advance and the rate is sometimes higher than the interest rate on your regular purchases.

Some people pay other bills with their credit card via cash advances and need to be aware that they are going to be paying a high interest rate with that move.

Borrowing From Peter to Pay Paul

Also, some people become so racked with debt that they make minimum payments and then immediately withdraw those payments as a cash advance so that they have that money to continue to live on. As you can see, it can become a never-ending cycle if you're not careful.

The Consequences of Minimum Payments

Credit cards are ok with you making minimum payments which is convenient to you and even more beneficial to them because the longer you carry your balance, the more money they will earn. Minimum payments are often less than 5% of the balance and because the interest rate on the card is most often much greater than that percentage, the card balance can get out of hand in no time.

If you let your spending get out of control and only make minimum payments, soon your balance will exceed your credit limit (if it hasn't already) and you'll probably be charged extra fees for going over the limit. Then there's interest on those late fees. It's easy to see how people can get into so much trouble with their credit cards.

Effective use of Credit Cards

Despite all the problems with credit cards, they can be useful. Not only can they be used to shop online and make reservations but you can get great perks as a result of using them such as loyalty program rewards including cash back rebates. The secret to using a credit card is to minimize the amount of interest you're paying by paying it off quickly.

You can get a low rate credit card and use it to pay off other bills at an interest rate that's less than what you are paying today. This would be good use of a credit card.

Parents often give their kids credit cards to help them in case of emergencies or to provide spending money. It's important that if this is the case, the parent teaches their child responsible spending and budgeting.

If you continue to use credit cards, be sure you review your statement every month and look at your spending trends as well as the interest you are paying. Strive to reduce your paid interest every month by cutting out things like cash advances and by making more than the minimum payment.

If you are using a credit card as a way to improve your credit rating, be very careful about the way that you use it.

Don't be afraid to ask your financial institution for a better deal than what you are getting today. If you run into problems, there are strategies for dealing with credit card debt that you can adopt. This will be covered in more detail later on in this book. The important thing is to realize that using a credit card is something you have to look at carefully. Weigh the costs of using that card for purchases by considering what the interest rate is and how much you'll actually be spending in the long run if you only make a partial payment.

4

Loans

There are many types of loans and many purposes for them. The principle of a loan is simple. Someone lends you money and you pay them back. For their trouble, there's an interest rate attached to the loan. You get to borrow money for something you need or want and the person with the money gets a little something for their trouble. Sounds pretty simple, right? The thing is, this can get people into a whole whack of debt.

There are many types of loans and they are used for many purposes.

Some of the reasons you might look to borrow money include:

- Buying a car
- Starting a business
- Make home improvements
- Buying a house
- Having a line of credit

- Consolidating Your Debts
- Going to school
- Some other reason
- Refinancing

Types of Loans

There are two basic types of loans and these are secured and unsecured loans.

Secured Loans

Secured loans require you to put something up for security in order to get the money. This is something that provides some protection from the lender so that if you default and do not pay, their risk is minimized by the collateral, which might be something such as your house or your car.

Unsecured Loans

Unsecured loans don't require any type of collateral. Only someone in a great financial position with a good credit history is likely to qualify for an unsecured loan of any high value. The lender looks at your income, your debts and your credit history with other creditors to determine whether or not you are credit worthy of an unsecured loan.

Payday Loans

A payday loan is something a little different than the traditional type of loan. A payday loan is a short-term loan that covers a need for a period no greater than the day you receive the funds to your next payday with your employer.

Payday loan lenders determine a rate you are qualified for based on what your paycheck is going to be for and charges an interest rate for providing the service. Generally they require that you write a post-dated check for your next payday to cover the principle and the interest. It's worthwhile to know that this is generally the highest rate of interest for any type of loan and as such, it's very easy to get into trouble with payday loans because paying back the loan requires such a big chunk of your pay. The payday loan trap is that many people use more than one payday loan place and continue to renew their loan each and every payday. As such, many people are in a vicious cycle of debt that equates to interest payments in the hundreds of dollars each month just to keep the debt going. Payday loans should be approached with extreme caution.

Applying for a loan

Applying for a loan is often as typical as applying for a credit card. There are applications to be completed and there is generally a waiting period while you wait to find out if you are approved or declined. If you apply for a loan with your own bank, you're often more likely to get approved because they know that they can simply deduct the payment from your account with them on a specific date each month.

For more complex loans like a business loan, you'll probably have to do more than fill out a one-page application. You'll probably need a business plan for that.

In the case of any loan, the lender is looking at you from the perspective of your ability to pay the loan back and what their recourse is if you do not, hence collateral. Sometimes you can apply for a loan and will be approved only if you have a co-signer.

Co-signers

A co-signer is someone who looks better on paper than you do. Perhaps your bank wants to give you a chance but isn't entirely convinced you can meet the requirements for qualifying for a loan. In this case, they may authorize a co-signer. That co-signer will have to apply for the loan and be considered liable if you default. It's a very big responsibility to have a loan and even bigger if you have a co-signer because the lender can deduct your missed loan payment from your co-signer's bank account and potential garnish their wages if you default.

Mortgages

Mortgages are loans that are taken out for the purpose of buying a home. It can be easier to get qualified for a mortgage than it is to get qualified for an unsecured line of credit or a credit card because the bank knows that if you default, they can take the house from you.

In most cases, you need to demonstrate credit worthiness and ability to pay when you apply for a mortgage. Based on your income and your down payment, you can get an approval for a specific amount of money. The bank or lender will have a list of things they need from you in order to qualify and generally you need to have all your ducks in a row on your credit report. This means that there can't be any bad debts that are not resolved on your report.

There are higher risk lenders and using these will require you to pay a higher interest rate so it's in your best interest to get your credit in good shape before applying for a mortgage. It could save you thousands of dollars.

Down Payments

Your mortgage amount is for your house price minus your down payment. Generally, a 5% to a 25% down payment is required but some banks will do 100% mortgage financing if you have stellar credit. Most banks want to know where the down payment is coming from and prefers to see that it is money you have saved for your house instead of cash advances from credit cards or loans. If you cannot make a down payment, you can also look at the option of a rent-to-own where a homeowner holds the mortgage and lets you add a down payment to the rent payment each month. This isn't the same as a regular mortgage and typically costs you extra.

Second Mortgages

A second mortgage is a loan taken with your house used as collateral. This is something people often do for things like home improvements or repairs or emergency expenses. It's important to be careful about a second mortgage because if you default on it, the lender can take your house from you even if the loan is for only a small amount.

Home equity loans

A home equity loan is somewhat like a second mortgage and provides you with a loan for an amount equal to the amount of equity you have in your home. Equity is the amount of money that you've paid towards your mortgage. It's important to note that your home equity is not the same as the amount you've paid on your mortgage so far. You need to subtract the interest first. When a mortgage is calculated, money collected from mortgage payments go to the interest payments before they go to the principal loan. So, if your mortgage is 1,000.00 a month and you've had your home for a year, you don't necessarily have $12,000 in equity. To determine what equity you do have, you need to minus the amount of interest payments you've made on your house so far.

Reverse Mortgage

A reverse mortgage is another form of equity stripping. It has become common for people in their retirement years who own their home and want to continue living in it but to have some of the money from the equity. When the house is sold, the reverse mortgage company takes their fees out of the sale of the house.

Consolidation Loans

A consolidation loan consolidates a bunch of debts into one loan. The reason this can be helpful is because a) you can have one payment to make a month instead of several which can be easier for budgeting purposes and b) you have one single interest rate instead of a bunch of different rates.

Consolidation loans work the best if you are cancelling the accounts the loan is created to consolidate. In other words, a consolidation loan only works for several credit cards if you cancel the credit cards after doing the consolidation. We'll look close at consolidation loans later in the refinancing and the debt reduction strategies chapters of this book.

Watching Your Debt Ratio

Loans can be convenient. They can help you get through tough times or buy something now and pay for it later. There are things we want and need that we just can't afford to pay for outright so paying a bit over time can be worthwhile. In the case of a mortgage, your appreciation rate of your home is likely to be much higher than your interest rate so that's considered a good debt. A consolidation loan is something that can also help you if you get a lowered interest rate but this is only helpful if you change your spending habits. Loans can also be dangerous. It's important to watch your debt ratio with mortgages and loans. It's vital to have a debt reduction plan and to live below your means so that you can save money for the future and have the ability to buy things with cash.

5

Refinancing

What is refinancing?

Refinancing is what people will do when they need to shuffle their debts around. There could be many reasons for this including:

- Lowering monthly payments

- Borrowing more money

- Consolidating debts

Lowering monthly payments might be a necessity when finances get out of control, borrowing more money might be needed and consolidating debts can be wise but with the caveat that consolidation is used as a chance to reduce debt load and interest and not as an opportunity to use more credit.

Refinancing a House

Refinancing is often done on cars and homes to stretch out the payments or to change lenders for various reasons including getting a better interest rate.

If you have a mortgage with only a few years of payments left, you might choose to refinance it so you can have a new loan. It's also common to take money out of your equity for investment purposes such as with planning for your retirement. Refinancing your house could also provide you with money to do repairs or improvements or to have money freed up from your equity to do other things with.

Refinancing your mortgage is the most common association to the word refinancing. Doing so can be helpful in terms of lowering your payment or changing the interest rate you are paying.

Refinancing a Car

For vehicles, if you're near to the end of your payment term but are having trouble making the payments you might choose to add a year to the loan and stretch the payments you have now over a longer period to create a lower monthly payment.

Refinancing Your Debts

Refinancing your debt can be a smart thing to do and is one of the most popular reasons for refinancing. If you find that your debts are difficult to manage, having a single creditor at one interest rate can be helpful. When refinancing your debts, the key thing is to save money on interest.

Pros and cons of Refinancing Your Home

There are pros and cons to refinancing anything and specifically your home. Your home is likely your most valuable asset so the sooner you have it paid off, the better.

But, because it's an asset it can be used as leverage so that you can qualify for loans, though. If you want to do something, using your home as leverage can help you achieve your goals.

Because the home is so valuable, it's something you don't want to lose so be very careful when refinancing your home in order to take equity out of it. Be careful about refinancing to make your payments smaller as well. Although this can feel like a good idea, it'll mean more interest payments made and it can mean a much higher debt ratio.

A good reason to refinance might be because you're moving from an adjustable rate mortgage to a fixed rate mortgage. This would definitely be a pro.

Cons resulting from that pro can include the fact that you might need to pay a penalty to your existing lender. Because the lender gave you a loan, they anticipated a specific amount of interest profit from your business so they may have a stipulation in your contract that states you will be required to pay a fee if you break the contract.

Fees might be associated with refinancing as well, which means you'll pay points to the new lender, which is a fee for doing the refinancing.

When you are looking at a refinancing contract, it's a good idea to look for one that doesn't require you to pay closing costs again. Most plans feature this option, which can prove to be a benefit of refinancing.

Where should you go for refinancing?

Banks and financial institutions offer this service and it's also common for agency services that help you find a refinancing partner to work for you.

Consolidation Loans

A consolidation loan is a way you can refinance your situation. By putting all your debts into one debt, you can lower you monthly payments, have a single payment instead of payments scattered throughout the month and you can relieve some financial stress and free up some cash flow.

One of the reasons people will consolidate is to help them before they get into trouble. Timing is everything with a consolidation loan. It's important to get the loan before you begin having trouble making payments because:

- You won't likely qualify for a consolidation loan if you're already one or two payments late on your debts and
- Timing can help you get out of trouble before it really begins.

The Secret to Consolidation Success

The secret to consolidation is to use it as a springboard to change your spending habits. It can be very helpful in reducing interest rates and taking away some stress.

Don't make the mistake of consolidating debts only to rack them up again otherwise you'll be in the same position as today a few months from now only it'll be worse because you'll be paying more interest rates and increasing your debt load to a point that becomes difficult to manage and you won't likely be able to consolidate yet again.

The secret to a consolidation loan is to use it to help you improve your financial situation and lighten the debt load while still working towards the goal of being debt free.

The mistake many people make is to use a consolidation loan to free the balances on credit cards so that they have the ability to use that credit again.

Credit Counselling

Credit counselling services can help people get a handle on their debts. When debts feel like they have spiralled out of control, it can be difficult to function. It can impact many areas of your life and cause health problems and depression. If you're having trouble getting by and feel like your debt is out of control, you should seek advice. This book offers very solid advice that can be very helpful. It can work alone to help you or work in conjunction with services.

What a Credit Counsellor Does

A credit counsellor can help you make a plan and a budget for future. They can also work with your creditors for you to come up with a plan to help you get your finances back on track.

Debt Repayment Plans

They might do a debt repayment plan, also known as a consumer proposal for you and get creditors to agree to lower interest rates or take smaller payments. What most often happens is that the debtor will pay a monthly payment they can afford to a credit-counselling agency and that agent will split the payments up between the creditors to help you pay down your debt.

Credit Counselling And Your Credit Report / Score

Credit counselling does show up on your credit report and is not a positive thing. However, it does help you and does bode better for you than a revolving bad debt on your credit report.

By dealing with credit counselling services, you can avoid wage garnishees and creditor calls as well as lower interest rates. This can be a good short-term solution until you are financially able to make larger payments. Most credit counselling services are non-profit agencies and only take a nominal fee for their services.

A credit counselling service will generally start off with an interview where they gather information about your situation and then they will contact you after they have spoken with your creditors.

Caution Regarding Credit Counselling

Be careful of services posing as credit counsellors that are not actually non-profit agencies. The fees involved in their doing things such as negotiating your debt or finding you refinancing options can be higher. Some companies prey on those who are naïve about their options and their rights with respect to their debts. Because debt management can feel overwhelming, it's easy to be scammed by someone who offers to take that heavy burden off your shoulders.

The Art of Negotiation

The credit counsellor uses negotiation skills. In all actuality, you have the power to do your own negotiating. You can contact your creditors and work out payment arrangements with them yourself. The next chapter will give you practical advice for dealing with your creditors and help you realize that you have leverage, even if you don't have much money in your pocket at the moment.

If you find it difficult or stressful to do this yourself, credit counselling can be a good option.

Refinancing Summary

In summary, refinancing can be a good thing. It can help you in different ways though so it's something you should approach carefully and be sure you become very knowledgeable about the plans you are making. If you are searching for someone to refinance with so you can get a lower interest rate, shop around. The better your credit rating is, the more leverage you have so it's worthwhile to pull your credit report before you take on refinancing to see how you look to others.

Many people take higher interest mortgages and loans in order to get credit to start off with and then once they look good on paper, they take their business elsewhere to an organization that is more eager to do business with them.

How you manage your debt load and your bills impacts not only your life today but also your future. The right decisions could put you in a very solid position financially and make you sought after by financial institutions that are practically falling over themselves to offer you money to lend.

6

Debt Collection

When you sign up for a new credit card or get money for a loan, you probably have every intention of paying it. When things get out of control and the debtors start getting aggressive, it gets difficult.

Beyond sending polite invoices and notices about your debts being owed and payments being late, creditors can get aggressive and it can get scary. It's important to try to deal with debt collection early. Believe it or not, the creditor wants to find an amicable solution for you both.

Tip:

Ignoring your creditors will just make things worse.

The following can begin happening:

- Harassing phone calls

- Visits
- Wage garnishment
- Repossession
- Foreclosure
- Court actions

Harassing Phone Calls

When debtors ignore their bills, the creditors will probably start to call. They will want to know what your intentions are with your debts and if you have a good history will likely be accommodating when you make a payment arrangement. You don't have to be harassed and you need to know your rights and exercise them if a creditor crosses the line. Rules and laws pertaining to their debt collection activities bind creditors.

Visits

Although this is not too common in this day and age, some creditors will visit your residence to inquire about collections. This might be the case if they are a local business that has the ability repossess goods you have purchased. This is common with rent-to-own furniture stores.

Foreclosure

Foreclosure on a mortgage can happen when you default on mortgage payments. Foreclosure has specific timelines and process of events depending on the terms set in your mortgage and where you live. It's vital that you are aware of your mortgage agreement and the terms listed in the default section of the agreement so you know how much breathing room you have on your mortgage payments.

Many agreements will state that if you miss two payments, you can go into default and lose your house. If you pay your mortgage weekly, you could lose your house in a matter of weeks instead of months so it's important to work closely with your lender if you are having problems making your payments.

Foreclosure is frightening. Because you have put so much money into your home, it's best to do everything you can to protect your investment. There are pre-foreclosure options you can exercise if you get stuck so that you don't lose all the money you have put into your home. As unfair as it may seem, if you are in the final year of a twenty-five year mortgage and get two payments behind, you could have to deal with foreclosure.

Repossession

If you have a car loan or a loan for furniture, it could be repossessed if you don't meet your payment obligations. You could have your vehicle repossessed at home or at work and it could be embarrassing or leave you in a bad situation if you wake up in the morning and your car is gone. Your creditor doesn't have to request your permission to repossess your vehicle if you don't meet the terms of your agreement with them.

Even if goods are repossessed, it's important for you to realize that you will still be liable for the costs you owe. Just because the items are removed from your possession doesn't mean that you are off the hook financially for money you owe for them.

Pay Garnishment

When a creditor is unsuccessful in getting their owed money from you, they may obtain a court order to begin garnishing your wages. Wage garnishment is a drastic measure but can happen if you are not careful.

Garnishment means that your employer will deduct an amount from your paycheck and send it directly to the court that will send the money to your creditor. This is a situation you'd obviously like to avoid if possible because it would mean that your employer gets involved in knowing your financial situation which could be both embarrassing as well as career limiting and the fact that a large chunk of your pay check could be taken from you.

Working with your Creditors

Making payments yourself is going to be easier than facing garnishment. Instead of losing something like 20% of your paycheck, you could make payments that are manageable for you.

Many creditors are willing to look at options that include:

- Deferring payments for you,
- Refinancing,
- Lowering the minimum payment and
- Lowering the interest rate.

They are more likely to be agreeable to negotiating terms if you deal with them early on rather than after several payments have been missed.

If you are in a situation where you are already several payments behind, you can still negotiate with the creditor at times. Let them know your situation and if they believe that bankruptcy is the only alternative if they don't work with you, they may be willing to make a deal.

It's important that you only make arrangements you feel you can meet. If you make a promise to make a payment, don't renege on that promise otherwise the creditor may not be willing to give you another opportunity.

If you work with your debtors, you can get out of debt. You might be surprised at what honesty does for taking the stress off you. Face the problems head on instead of ignoring them.

Debts won't go away by themselves unless you're prepared to hide for up to seven years when they will eventually disappear from your credit report and life in the meantime could be pretty difficult if that's what you choose to do.

Your Rights

Despite missing payments, you have rights and needn't be treated like a second-class citizen. You do not have to be poorly treated by creditors and they have roles and responsibilities. Knowing your rights is important. Your local government will have guidelines set that the creditors have to follow. The creditor is not allowed to humiliate you publicly, they are not allowed to threaten you or excessively harass you.

They are allowed to lawfully collect their money and if you believe that a creditor is treating you unlawfully, you can take action. Your creditor cannot harass you at work if it could cause problems with your employment status and should not attempt to contact you at inconvenient hours (such as the middle of the night.) They cannot make false statements and should not use profane or obscene language with you.

You have the right to officially request that the creditor ceases contacting you. If this happens, they will typically take legal action such as obtaining a court judgment, garnishing wages or repossession instead of trying to collect.

You can contact the attorney general's office or your local consumer protection agency and you can also file for damages if the creditor does not follow guidelines and this causes you financial loss. Letting an aggressive creditor know that you are well aware of your rights can be very helpful.

Helpful Resources:

USA - Fair Debt Collection
http://www.ftc.gov/bcp/edu/pubs/consumer/credit/cre18.shtm

Canada - Dealing With Debt: A Consumer Guide
http://strategis.ic.gc.ca/epic/site/bsf-osb.nsf/en/br01035e.html

UK – Managing Debt
http://www.direct.gov.uk/en/MoneyTaxAndBenefits/ManagingDebt/index.htm

A glance at filing bankruptcy

Bankruptcy is a detailed process and an entire book could be devoted to it so this section merely presents a glance at bankruptcy. Hopefully you are not in a position where things seem hopeless enough to declare bankruptcy. It is an option for some people, though and a chance to start again with many lessons learned.

Bankruptcy doesn't just happen because people make poor choices about their finances. Sometimes things out of our control happen such as a death in the family, an illness, a layoff or a failing business.

It's important to know that if you suffer bankruptcy, you can start again. After you are discharged, you can begin to rebuild your credit.

Bankruptcy Procedures

Filing bankruptcy happens when it has been determined that there is no way out of your current level of debt and you cannot pay it back.

When you file bankruptcy, you're considered insolvent. Different countries have varying rules about how bankruptcy works but for illustration purposes, let's look at the United States. After you've decided which bankruptcy trustee to work with, your process begins.

Some bankruptcy proceedings allow you to keep certain property such as your home. Others result in your losing your home. Speak to a trustee about your specific circumstances but if you are able to continue making payments, your home and car may be exempt from bankruptcy.

1. Means Test. A test is performed to determine if you qualify to declare bankruptcy. This is a long test that has you answer questions about your specific financial circumstances.

2. Documentation is filed.

3. Credit counselling classes are attended. This is an effort to get your debts resolved without bankruptcy. After this class, bankruptcy can be resumed unless you are able to come to an agreement.

4. Court filings then take place and you attend a meeting as a formality to close things off.

5. After your court hearing you will need to attend a budgeting class that's mandatory and meet other requirements that will allow you to become discharged from bankruptcy.

Some money will need to be paid to creditors and you will have to sign over income tax refunds as well during the bankruptcy period. You may have to make a small monthly payment for a specified amount of time. Certain debts may not be covered by bankruptcy so may still need to be repaid.

Chapter Review:

In dealing with your creditors to resolve your debts, the most important advice you can get is that communication is key and negotiation is almost always possible.

Whether you're talking to a utility company, a credit card company or the mortgage holder for your home, if you are honest and up front and do your best to work with your creditors instead of against them by hiding and ignoring their calls, you can likely come up with a workable solution.

Sometimes a creditor will take a partial payment or might even refer you to a service that can help you such as a special government fund for electricity bills. Some governments prevent electricity from being turned off in the winter or have programs that help people with specific problems.

Sometimes a creditor will refer you to a credit counselling service as well.

Credit counselling can be a helpful option if you feel you are over your head and can relieve a lot of stress.

Bankruptcy is an option but it's important that you exhaust all other alternatives before deciding to file bankruptcy. It could be that some creative budgeting and self discipline plus hard work could get you back on track financially in a short time.

7

Strategies to Help You Reduce Your Debt

How do you know if it's time to do something about your finances?

Ask yourself the following questions:

- Am I ignoring phone calls because I'm afraid it's a creditor calling?
- Am I borrowing from Peter to pay Paul on a regular basis?
- Do I use credit cards for things like groceries?
- Do I get regular disconnection notices on my utilities?
- How much am I paying on late fees because I haven't paid my bills on time?
- Do I follow a budget?
- Do I even have a budget?
- Is the state of my money causing relationship problems for me?

- Is the state of my finances keeping me awake at night?

If you've answered yes to more of these questions than no, it's time to make some changes.

As discussed in the last chapter, facing your debts head on is important. Not only will the problems not go away by themselves but they will get worse because your creditors will take actions. Worse than worrying about what will happen is being eyeball deep in having action taken against you.

So if you're now in a state of bad debts, you're happy to have arrived at this chapter because the last several have probably reminded you of some mistakes you've made.

If you're not in a bad situation yet but see it on the horizon, this chapter can help you tackle your problems head on and help you reduce stress. And finally, if you're learning about debts and finance for the safety of your own financial future, good for you for taking the steps to develop good financial habits.

The knowledge in this book can help you learn from others and help you start off with financial habits that can help you make a solid investment in your own future.

How do you get on track?

1. Follow a budget
2. Change your spending habits
3. Live Below your means
4. Negotiate
5. Plan for the future

Change Your Spending Habits

Today we live in a society that is very accustomed to spending money like it is going out of style. Brand names are a status symbol and debit cards and credit cards make it so easy to spend without thinking about the consequences of that spending. Put yourself on a cash budget and keep track of your spending.

By using cash, you can get a handle on your spending. Keep your receipts, do regular analysis of your spending and financial situation and set short term and long-term goals.

Follow a budget

In your budget you need to do more than just plan for today. You need to be thinking of tomorrow as well. You need to:

- Have money for day-to-day expenses,
- Put money away for emergencies,
- Have money for the future (i.e. savings)

- And pay down your debt.

Following a budget is what can help you with your debt. It takes some planning and a large amount of discipline but can make a massive difference in your life.

Soon after seeing the positive results of a budget, you'll find more creative ways to save money and while it might feel constricting at first because you can't just buy whatever you like any longer, in no time you'll find it liberating because you'll be stress-free, debt-free and have more money in the long run to do things you want instead of wasting money away on consumables.

There are budgeting software packages you can buy that can help you track your spending and plan your finances. Some packages even offer built-in income tax packages to help you really manage your finances. You might even own a budgeting software package already bundled with your computer system and now could be a great time to play with it.
If you don't want to invest quite yet, you can start off by making a simple spreadsheet on your computer that will help you manage your budget.

A sample budget could list the following:

Fixed Expenses

1. Rent or Mortgage
2. Insurance Payments
3. Fixed utility bills
4. Fixed loan payments

Variable expenses

1. Groceries
2. Car maintenance
3. Gas
4. Clothing
5. Gifts
6. Entertainment
7. Bill payments

There are also other expenses you should consider such as:

1. Emergency fund
2. Paying down debt
3. Savings

Some people also keep a fund of "mad money". This can be money left over from your saving efforts or from extra income such as overtime or online income from e-bay or doing a part-time job.

When you pay your bills, you need to try to pay more than the minimum payment. In order to reduce your debt, it's a good idea to allocate extra money to one bill until it is paid off. If you think of debt reduction in the shape of a pyramid, this can be helpful. The bill at the top gets paid off and then the extra money you have after that bill is eliminated means that the money trickles down to the next set of bills. You could also do it like a totem pole and pay down one bill at a time.

Then, when the bill is gone, instead of spending that money you would have put towards that bill, add the money to another bill payment to get that debt paid off and so on. In a short time, you could have absolutely no debt.

Tip:

Put the bill with the highest interest rate at the top of your debt repayment pyramid (or totem pole) and allocate other bills in priority sequence based on their interest rate.

Sample Budget

Family Budget

Total Earnings	Spouse 1	$	2,500.00
	Spouse 2	$	1,200.00
	Total:	$	3,700.00

Bills Static

	Monthly	
Mortgage	$	1,000.00
Phone	$	100.00
Insurance	$	150.00
Car Payment	$	300.00
Loan Payment	$	200.00
Internet	$	20.00
Hydro	$	200.00
Banking Fees	$	15.00
Total	$	1,985.00

Variable Bills

	Monthly		Weekly	
Food	$	500.00	$	125.00
Gas	$	100.00	$	25.00
Medicine	$	50.00	$	12.50
Entertainment	$	20.00	$	5.00
Clothing and Gifts	$	20.00	$	5.00
Misc	$	100.00	$	25.00
Total:	$	790.00	$	197.50

Debts

Credit Card 1	$	1,000.00
Credit Card 2	$	2,000.00
Credit Card 3	$	3,000.00
total:	$	6,000.00

Debt Repayment Schedule

	Card 1	Card 2	Card 3
Month 1	$ 200.00	$ 200.00	$ 200.00
Month 2	$ 200.00	$ 200.00	$ 200.00
Month 3	$ 200.00	$ 200.00	$ 200.00
Month 4	$ 200.00	$ 200.00	$ 200.00
Month 5	$ 200.00	$ 200.00	$ 200.00
Month 6	$ -	$ 400.00	$ 200.00
Month 7	$ -	$ 400.00	$ 200.00
Month 8	$ -	$ 200.00	$ 400.00
Month 9	$ -	$ -	$ 600.00
Month 10	$ -	$ -	$ 600.00
Month 11	$ -	$ -	$ -
Month 12	$ -	$ -	$ -
Total:	$ 1,000.00	$ 2,000.00	$ 3,000.00

In this budget system, you can easily see how things break down and budget accordingly. In order to budget you need to understand how much you earn, what your debts are and how to make a variable expense budget.

In the debt repayment schedule, you can see that you can become debt free in less than a year in a scenario like the above. To pay off minimum credit card payments would result in years of payments and a lot of interest. This budget doesn't illustrate interest rates but it's easy to see that instead of taking years to pay off your debts, if you organize a budget, you can become debt free and have money in the bank to spare.

The Envelope System

How do you manage the money you spend on flexible expenses? This is the typical danger zone in terms of managing your money because people spend thousands of dollars each month and can't account for where it has gone.

The envelope or money jar system is a great way to manage your spending. Use jars or envelopes and categorise them for your spending. By doing this, you can ensure that you will stay within your budget.

Classify your flexible expenses like food, gas, entertainment and spending money by creating an envelope or jar for each category. When you set your budget for the week, place the allotted amount into the labelled envelope.

Don't allow yourself to spend more than this amount of money. Be sure to save one for emergencies and each week, whatever is left in the envelopes can move to either an emergency fund, to savings or to give you an extra treat such as going out for dinner, buying something fun or having a bit more breathing room.

Here are some suggestions for categories:

- Food
- Gas
- Medicine
- Entertainment
- Clothing and Gifts
- Miscellaneous

Put the weekly allotment into each jar and stick to the budget. If you look at the sample budget above, you can see that a division was made listing the weekly budget as well as the monthly budget. Dividing variable expenses by week can show you how much money to place in your jars.

If you can make the money stretch, you're on your way to following a budget. This might mean that you spend $100 a week on groceries instead of $200 or that you only allow your family to go to eat in a restaurant once a month and could mean a movie rental at the video store for your weekly entertainment instead of a night out at the movies.

At first those envelopes will empty quickly but before you know it, you could have money left over at the end of the week.

Many people who follow the envelope system swear by it and enjoy the challenge of managing their money this way. By using cash and seeing where it goes, it makes it much harder to overspend. It changes your mentality about spending.

Here's the kicker:

Tip:

By spending cash, you know what you are spending. Debit cards often have service charges and credit cards have hefty interest fees. When you spend cash, you are putting more money into your own pocket and getting more value for your money and here's a big tip: cash equals buying power.

Try testing out this theory:

The next time you want to buy a big ticket item like a new television, furniture or a used car, see how much more negotiating power you have in a small store with cash in your hand instead of looking to either sign up for their credit event or put it on your credit card. You can save huge amounts of money with cash because small retailers like to have money now rather than wait for the credit cards to send them checks or wait for financing companies who charge a fee for performing financial services.

Determining Your Variable Spending Budget

After you've done a budget of what you have coming in and what must go out automatically with fixed expenses, figure out what you have left over and divide it among your flexible expenses. If there is less money than what you expect, it's time to trim your spending. Also, there should be money left over for debt reduction and savings. Even if that's only a small amount of money, that's a start but if you're having trouble balancing your budget, you need to figure out how to reduce your expenses.

Tough Decisions

Sometimes you have to make tough decisions in order to balance your budget. This might mean selling an expensive car, moving to a cheaper home or dramatically reducing your spending money. It's a hard thing to do at first but will be short-term sacrifice for long-term gain.

Live Below your means

You don't want to live above your means or even at your means. We discussed this earlier but it bears repeating.

Above your means would be that you are spending more a month than you bring in. It's not difficult to do but it is a challenging habit to break. Society has become very credit driven and while credit can be a good thing, it an also be very devastating if you live too far out of your means.

Living at your means is living paycheck to paycheck. If you have exactly enough money to live on and no more and no less, you won't be able to do things you want or prepare for your future.

The goal is to live below your means so that there is not more month than there is money and so that you can handle a financial crisis because you are prepared.

If you think back to your Grandmother's spending habits, she probably used a system like the envelope system and probably had a cookie jar or piggy bank that she used to save up for things like new things for the home or family vacations. The obsolescence of this type of mentality of waiting until we can afford something before we buy it is what is causing the climbing debt rates and increased instances of bankruptcy filings.

Negotiate

The art of negotiating is not lost. It means that when you spend your money, you look for the best deal. A big part of budgeting is saving money and if you look at your spending habits today, there are probably many areas where you can negotiate your finances better.

This might mean doing some more shopping around before you buy something, waiting until it goes on sale or talking to a creditor about lowering your interest rate. It also means talking to your creditors when you have problems so you can come to an amicable agreement. Own your debts instead of letting your debt own you and run your life. Plan for the future.

Plan for the future

There will come a day that your income dramatically decreases. Hopefully you are planning for your retirement but in the mean time, are you prepared for a financial emergency that could happen long before then?

Many things can happen to put you in financial jeopardy so it's important to have a plan. Saving money for a rainy day is important. If you're a homeowner, you need an emergency fund for house repairs. If you live somewhere that doesn't have national healthcare, you don't want an injury to ruin your family's finances. You might be assuming you cannot afford to buy life insurance but perhaps you have a $50 a month Starbucks habit. If that's the case, it's time to make some changes.

Every little bit counts so when you do your budgeting plan, do your best to save some money. Whether you see a financial planner and cook up a great scheme to invest and earn or simply open a high interest account to transfer money to every payday, every little bit will help.

Tip:

When you do your budget, allow for money to go into savings. If you have trouble with this, budget for that savings as a fixed expense and consider having it come automatically off your paycheck so that you budget for living without it and don't miss the money.

Many companies who do direct deposit of your pay into your bank account will let you split your pay so you could put five or ten per cent or even $50 per payday into a separate account. It's a great idea to make that account a little bit difficult to access.

You want to be able to access the money if you need it but perhaps you don't need a debit card for it. If you have to line up in the bank during regular banking hours in order to access the money, you are less likely to spend it.

Conclusion

Money definitely does make the world go round. You have the ability, even if you have a somewhat limited income to grow your personal wealth. If you're in serious debt today, you can turn things around.

There are going to be ups and downs in your finances throughout your life and careful consideration, planning and saving for a rainy day are three essential elements to good finance.